Francis Frith's

North Wales

Photographic Memories

Francis Frith's

North Wales

Revised and enlarged edition of an
original work by

Helen Livingston

First published in the United Kingdom in 1998 by
Waterton Press Ltd

Paperback Edition 2001
ISBN 1-85937-298-8

Hardback Edition 2001
ISBN 1-85937-361-5

Reprinted in paperback 2003

British Library Cataloguing in Publication Data

Francis Frith's North Wales
Revised & enlarged edition of an
original work by Helen Livingston

Frith Book Company Ltd
Frith's Barn, Teffont,
Salisbury, Wiltshire SP3 5QP
Tel: +44 (0) 1722 716 376
Email: info@francisfrith.co.uk
www.francisfrith.co.uk

Printed and bound in Great Britain

Front Cover: Barmouth, High Street 1908 60215

AS WITH ANY HISTORICAL DATABASE THE FRITH ARCHIVE IS CONSTANTLY BEING CORRECTED AND IMPROVED
AND THE PUBLISHERS WOULD WELCOME INFORMATION ON OMISSIONS OR INACCURACIES
Please note: The original spellings from *F Frith & Co* ledgers for some Welsh place names have been retained
for the purposes of historical accuracy

Contents

Francis Frith: *Victorian Pioneer*

FRANCIS FRITH, Victorian founder of the world-famous photographic archive, was a complex and multi-talented man. A devout Quaker and a highly successful Victorian businessman, he was both philosophic by nature and pioneering in outlook.

By 1855 Francis Frith had already established a wholesale grocery business in Liverpool, and sold it for the astonishing sum of £200,000, which is the equivalent today of over £15,000,000. Now a multi-millionaire, he was able to indulge his passion for travel. As a child he had pored over travel books written by early explorers, and his fancy and imagination had been stirred by family holidays to the sublime mountain regions of Wales and Scotland. 'What a land of spirit-stirring and enriching scenes and places!' he had written. He was to return to these scenes of grandeur in later years to 'recapture the thousands of vivid and tender memories', but with a different purpose. Now in his thirties, and captivated by the new science of photography, Frith set out on a series of pioneering journeys to the Nile regions that occupied him from 1856 until 1860.

Intrigue and Adventure

He took with him on his travels a specially-designed wicker carriage that acted as both dark-room and sleeping chamber. These far-flung journeys were packed with intrigue and adventure. In his life story, written when he was sixty-three, Frith tells of being held captive by bandits, and of fighting 'an awful midnight battle to the very point of surrender with a deadly pack of hungry, wild dogs'. Sporting flowing Arab costume, Frith arrived at Akaba by camel seventy years before Lawrence, where he encountered 'desert princes and rival sheikhs, blazing with jewel-hilted swords'.

During these extraordinary adventures he was assiduously exploring the desert regions bordering the Nile and patiently recording the antiquities and peoples with his camera. He was the first photographer to venture beyond the sixth cataract. Africa was still the mysterious 'Dark Continent', and Stanley and Livingstone's historic meeting was a decade into the future. The conditions for picture taking confound belief. He laboured for hours in his wicker dark-room in the sweltering heat of the desert, while the volatile chemicals fizzed dangerously in their trays. Often he was forced to work in remote tombs and caves where conditions were cooler. Back in London he exhibited his photographs and was 'rapturously cheered' by members of the Royal Society. His reputation as a photographer was made overnight. An eminent modern historian has likened their impact on the population of the time to that on our own generation of the first photographs taken on the surface of the moon.

Venture of a Life-Time

Characteristically, Frith quickly spotted the opportunity to create a new business as a specialist publisher of photographs. He lived in an era of immense and sometimes violent change. For the poor in the early part of Victoria's reign work was a drudge and the hours long, and people had precious little free time to enjoy themselves. Most had no transport other than a cart or gig at their disposal, and had not travelled far beyond the boundaries of their own town or village. However,

by the 1870s, the railways had threaded their way across the country, and Bank Holidays and half-day Saturdays had been made obligatory by Act of Parliament. All of a sudden the ordinary working man and his family were able to enjoy days out and see a little more of the world.

With characteristic business acumen, Francis Frith foresaw that these new tourists would enjoy having souvenirs to commemorate their days out. In 1860 he married Mary Ann Rosling and set out with the intention of photographing every city, town and village in Britain. For the next thirty years he travelled the country by train and by pony and trap, producing fine photographs of seaside resorts and beauty spots that were keenly bought by millions of Victorians. These prints were painstakingly pasted into family albums and pored over during the dark nights of winter, rekindling precious memories of summer excursions.

The Rise of Frith & Co

Frith's studio was soon supplying retail shops all over the country. To meet the demand he gathered about him a small team of photographers, and published the work of independent artist-photographers of the calibre of Roger Fenton and Francis Bedford. In order to gain some understanding of the scale of Frith's business one only has to look at the catalogue issued by Frith & Co in 1886: it runs to some 670 pages, listing not only many thousands of views of the British Isles but also many photographs of most European countries, and China, Japan, the USA and Canada — note the sample page shown above from the hand-written *Frith & Co* ledgers detailing pictures taken. By 1890 Frith had created the greatest specialist photographic publishing company in the world,

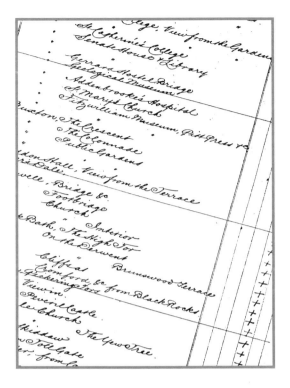

with over 2,000 outlets – more than the combined number that Boots and WH Smith have today! The picture on the right shows the *Frith & Co* display board at Ingleton in the Yorkshire Dales. Beautifully constructed with mahogany frame and gilt inserts, it could display up to a dozen local scenes.

Postcard Bonanza

The ever-popular holiday postcard we know today took many years to develop. In 1870 the Post Office issued the first plain cards, with a pre-printed stamp on one face. In 1894 they allowed other publishers' cards to be sent through the mail with an attached adhesive halfpenny stamp. Demand grew rapidly, and in 1895 a new size of postcard was permitted called the court card, but there was little room for illustration. In 1899, a year after

Frith's death, a new card measuring 5.5 x 3.5 inches became the standard format, but it was not until 1902 that the divided back came into being, with address and message on one face and a full-size illustration on the other. *Frith & Co* were in the vanguard of postcard development, and Frith's sons Eustace and Cyril continued their father's monumental task, expanding the number of views offered to the public and recording more and more places in Britain, as the coasts and countryside were opened up to mass travel.

Francis Frith died in 1898 at his villa in Cannes, his great project still growing. The archive he created continued in business for another seventy years. By 1970 it contained over a third of a million pictures of 7,000 cities, towns and villages. The massive photographic record Frith has left to us stands as a living monument to a special and very remarkable man.

Frith's Archive: *A Unique Legacy*

FRANCIS FRITH'S legacy to us today is of immense significance and value, for the magnificent archive of evocative photographs he created provides a unique record of change in 7,000 cities, towns and villages throughout Britain over a century and more. Frith and his fellow studio photographers revisited locations many times down the years to update their views, compiling for us an enthralling and colourful pageant of British life and character.

We tend to think of Frith's sepia views of Britain as nostalgic, for most of us use them to conjure up memories of places in our own lives with which we have family associations. It often makes us forget that to Francis Frith they were records of daily life as it was actually being lived in the cities, towns and villages of his day. The Victorian age was one of great and often bewildering change for ordinary people, and though the pictures evoke an impression of slower times, life was as busy and hectic as it is today.

We are fortunate that Frith was a photographer of the people, dedicated to recording the minutiae of everyday life. For it is this sheer wealth of visual data, the painstaking chronicle of changes in dress, transport, street layouts, buildings, housing, engineering and landscape that captivates us so much today. His remarkable images offer us a powerful link with the past and with the lives of our ancestors.

Today's Technology

Computers have now made it possible for Frith's many thousands of images to be accessed almost instantly. In the Frith archive today, each photograph is carefully 'digitised' then stored on a CD Rom. Frith archivists can locate a single photograph amongst thousands within seconds. Views can be catalogued and sorted under a variety of categories of place and content to the immediate benefit of researchers.

Inexpensive reference prints can be created for them at the touch of a mouse button, and a wide range of books and other printed materials assembled and published for a wider, more general readership - in the next twelve months over a hundred Frith local history titles will be published! The day-to-day workings of the archive are very different from how they were in Francis Frith's time: imagine the herculean task of sorting through eleven tons of glass negatives as Frith had to do to locate a particular sequence of pictures! Yet

See Frith at www.francisfrith.co.uk

the archive still prides itself on maintaining the same high standards of excellence laid down by Francis Frith, including the painstaking cataloguing and indexing of every view.

It is curious to reflect on how the internet now allows researchers in America and elsewhere greater instant access to the archive than Frith himself ever enjoyed. Many thousands of individual views can be called up on screen within seconds on one of the Frith internet sites, enabling people living continents away to revisit the streets of their ancestral home town, or view places in Britain where they have enjoyed holidays. Many overseas researchers welcome the chance to view special theme selections, such as transport, sports, costume and ancient monuments.

We are certain that Francis Frith would have heartily approved of these modern developments in imaging techniques, for he himself was always working at the very limits of Victorian photographic technology.

The Value of the Archive Today

Because of the benefits brought by the computer, Frith's images are increasingly studied by social historians, by researchers into genealogy and ancestory, by architects, town planners, and by teachers and schoolchildren involved in local history projects.

In addition, the archive offers every one of us an opportunity to examine the places where we and our families have lived and worked down the years. Highly successful in Frith's own era, the archive is now, a century and more on, entering a new phase of popularity.

The Past in Tune with the Future

Historians consider the Francis Frith Collection to be of prime national importance. It is the only archive of its kind remaining in private ownership and has been valued at a million pounds. However, this figure is now rapidly increasing as digital technology enables more and more people around the world to enjoy its benefits.

Francis Frith's archive is now housed in an historic timber barn in the beautiful village of Teffont in Wiltshire. Its founder would not recognize the archive office as it is today. In place of the many thousands of dusty boxes containing glass plate negatives and an all-pervading odour of photographic chemicals, there are now ranks of computer screens. He would be amazed to watch his images travelling round the world at unimaginable speeds through network and internet lines.

The archive's future is both bright and exciting. Francis Frith, with his unshakeable belief in making photographs available to the greatest number of people, would undoubtedly approve of what is being done today with his lifetime's work. His photographs, depicting our shared past, are now bringing pleasure and enlightenment to millions around the world a century and more after his death.

Barmouth and the South

Extract from Barmouth 1898 21696

Aberdovey, The front 1895 36507
This small seaside town on the west coast overlooks the wide sandy expanse of the Dyfi estuary. It is sheltered from the north wind by hills rising to the sombre Welsh mountains south of Cadair Idris. Today it is popular for watersports, but formerly it was an important sea port. The coastal trade was very important to Aberdyfi during the 19th century; earlier, smuggling had been rife. This picture of the front shows a cargo vessel and numerous small fishing boats beached opposite the church.

Aberdovey, From the Hills 1892 30243
St Peter's, the Victorian church in the middle of the picture, was Aberdovey (or Aberdyfi's) first church, though the song 'The Bells of Aberdyfi' suggests that an earlier church lies drowned beneath the waves of Cardigan Bay. The gardens rise steeply behind the cottages, the irregular plots divided by walls and unkempt shrubs.

Aberdovey, The Seafront 1892 30248
In this view of the seafront just west of the harbour, a lone wagon stands on the siding from the Aberdovey Harbour branch line. The seafront terraces and hills behind remain much the same today, and boating has grown ever more popular in the Dyfi estuary, which is fringed by wooded banks.

Aberdovey, From the Sands 1901 46977
This view looks across the broad expanse of firm sands to a goods train, which is probably carrying slate on the now-vanished harbour branch of the railway. Many of the terraces would have been built by local speculators as lodgings for visitors - the mildness and salubriousness of the climate made the town popular as a winter residence.

Aberdovey, The Harbour 1901 46976
Three tall ships are visible; the one on the far left is just setting sail. The town relied on the sea for employment, and it was once an important rival of Holyhead for the Irish ferry. The seafront houses create a pleasing harmony, the result of the efforts down the years of individual architects and owners, unlike in the previous photograph.

▼ **Towyn, The View from Marine Parade 1908** 60255
This seaside resort on the Cardigan Bay coast shelters behind its sand dunes and wide sandy beach. Its reputation as a watering-place was founded on the exceptional purity of its air and water. It is home to the Tal-y-Llyn Railway, which opened in 1865, making it the oldest narrow-gauge railway in Wales; it brought slate down from the Abergynolwyn quarries. This photograph looks south along the sandy beach, which stretches for some three miles.

▼ **Towyn, High Street, from the Station 1895** 36494
We are looking eastwards into the Welsh mountains along the high street from the railway bridge. The entrance to the mainline station can be seen on the right, while the tower of St Cadfan's church is clearly visible in the centre of the picture. This church is one of the most interesting in Wales. It is cruciform, with a Norman nave, aisles and north transept. St Cadfan was one of the Three Blessed Visitors who came from Brittany in the 6th century; he was the founder and first abbot of the monastery on Bardsey Island.

▲ **Towyn, College Green 1901** 46989
The green was at the heart of the old village. The tower of the Norman church of St Cadfan stands in the centre. The church was restored and partly rebuilt in 1882. The 7th-century St Cadfan's Stone, in the church, is thought to bear the earliest example of written Welsh. Adjoining the churchyard is St Cadfan's Well, in which Giraldus Cambrensis bathed on his pilgrimage through Wales in 1180.

◄ **Towyn, High Street
1908** 60259
Towyn (or Tywyn) means
both 'an extent of land' and
'a thing that shines', a good
description of the sand and
marsh around the town.
This photograph shows the
deserted High Street on a
day of bright sunlight, with
the summit of Pen Trum-gwr
looming ahead, and the
modest Edwards
Commercial Hotel and
Boarding House on the left.
The view is little changed
today.

Abergynolwyn, The Dysynni Valley 1895
36487
This former slate-mining village lies below Cadair Idris, cupped in the Dysynni valley between Tal y Llyn and Tywyn. It was served by the narrow gauge Tal-y-Llyn railway, the first of the slate railways of North Wales to be preserved. The railway runs inland from Tywyn on the Cardigan Bay coast. This evocative view shows the valley downstream of Abergynolwyn. The river can be seen at the bottom of the steep slope on the left. The house opposite is Nant Myniawyd.

Abergynolwyn, General View 1968 A12012
There is little apart from the Mini van parked in front of the terraced house on the bottom right of the picture to give away the date of this view, which looks north over Abergynolwyn. The village sits in its valley partly in the parish of Tal-y-llyn and partly in Llanfihangel. Most of its cottages would have been lived in by quarrymen, who laboured in the Bryneglwys slate quarry, long since closed.

Tal-y-llyn, The Lake 1937 88048
In translation, Tal-y-Llyn means 'the end of the lake': that aptly describes the location of the village, with its little church and inns in the shadow of Cadair Idris. It sits at the south-western end of the lake, where the River Dysynni comes tumbling out in a series of little cascades. The lake has always been famous for trout fishing. This view of Tal-y-Llyn lake - Llyn Mwyngil in Welsh - looks much the same today, with the slopes of Cadair Idris rising up on the left. On the right-hand shore the B4405 snakes along towards Cross Foxes and Dolgellau.

Machynlleth, The Corris Railway 1899 44555
Corris, which gave its name to the Welsh narrow-gauge railway line, is a slate-quarrying village in the valley of the Afon Dulas. Slates are used here not just for roofing but for numerous other purposes, including fencing. The narrow gauge railway ran from Machynlleth to Corris. It was opened in 1859 and closed, following flooding, in 1948. This locomotive is now used on the Tal-y-Llyn railway.

◀ **Dolgellau, From the Station 1888** 20794
This view, taken from the station, shows the town and Cadair Idris, the River Wnion, the famous 17th-century bridge and tollhouse, and the tower of St Mary's church. The scene has been obliterated by time - the railway shut down in 1965, and the A494 has been rebuilt through the centre of the picture.

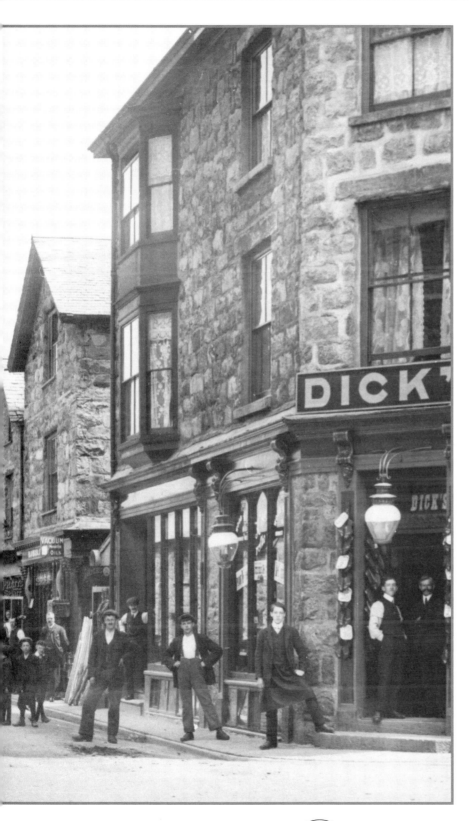

Dolgellau, Upper Smithfield Street 1908 60243

Dolgellau was the county town of the old county of Merioneth, and is set amid the mountains which are famous for Welsh gold - the mines here provided gold for Royal wedding rings. From the mid 17th century there was a strong Quaker presence in Dolgellau. Here, shopkeepers, their families and employees pose for the photographer; note Dick's display of shoes on the right. A motor car can be seen in the centre of the picture, driven by a uniformed chauffeur. This is the 20th century, after all, and sophisticated technology is here to stay. Yet a shop on the right has yokes for dairy maids and farm workers for sale - medieval equipment is still here as well.

Dolgellau, Market Square 1930 83598
The town's arcaded Market House of 1870 stands in the Square. The local dark building stone has given Dolgellau much of its character. The town was a centre for the manufacture of flannels, coarse woollen cloths and kerseys. Currying and tanning were also carried on. The Midland Bank, on the right, is a typically self-important building.

Arthog, From across the Estuary 1889 21755
This view looks south-east across the Mawddach estuary saltings towards the village, which lies on the south shore. The great bulk of Cadair Idris rises behind it. The old Barmouth-Llangollen railway line is visible across the middle of the picture.

Barmouth
From the Breakwater 1889 21696

This well-known holiday resort, which has an excellent sandy
beach, stands on the west coast of Wales at the mouth of the
Mawddach estuary. Both Darwin and Ruskin enjoyed stays here.
The old harbour stands on the shores of the Mawddach estuary,
and was formerly of some importance. Nearby, the viewpoint of
Dinas Oleu was the National Trust's first property. This beautifully-
composed view looks back to the town from the breakwater. The
old town clings to the steep hillside, and the beginning of the
famous Barmouth Bridge is visible on the right.

Barmouth, The Railway Bridge 1896

37685

This famous bridge spans the Mawddach estuary. A train is heading south. The railway was built as part of the Cambrian railway, with two stations, Barmouth and Barmouth Junction. Northwards the line went to Harlech and Afonwen, where it joined the L & NWR. The bridge was opened in September 1867 and its original design, as shown in this picture, included rolling sections that could be opened for river traffic to sail through. It is 800 yards long and has a road for foot passengers, who can enjoy the freshness of the air and the sublime vistas of Cadair Idris.

◄ **Barmouth, The Railway Bridge 1908**
60208
This shows the 2,253ft long bridge with a train heading north. It was constructed primarily of wood, except for the section that passes over the river bed, which is of iron girders and pile-driven steel cylinders. The rolling sections visible in photograph No 37685 were replaced in 1899 by an iron swing bridge.

◄ Barmouth, A View from the Hills 1892

30195

This splendid view of the town shows Ty'r Graig Castle Hotel in the foreground. It is still smothered in scaffolding, but is nearing completion. The shape of this unique building was designed to represent a double-barrelled shotgun.

▼ Barmouth, High Street 1908

60216

Holiday makers walk the high street, and a coach and four is about to pull up outside the Cors-y-Cedol Hotel, one of the resort's many hotels. The passengers sitting out on top must have had to hang onto their fine hats in the breezy air of the estuary. St Ann's Hotel, on the other side of the road, advertises medical, physical and therapeutic benefits.

◄ Barmouth, Marine Parade 1913 65880

Here we see the town's newly-built lodging houses and seaside villas, with an early motor car on the left in front of the Belgrave Hotel. Well-dressed holidaymakers stroll along the seafront. In the foreground is a wicker-work bathchair - many convalescents and elderly people would have come to the town for a soothing holiday.

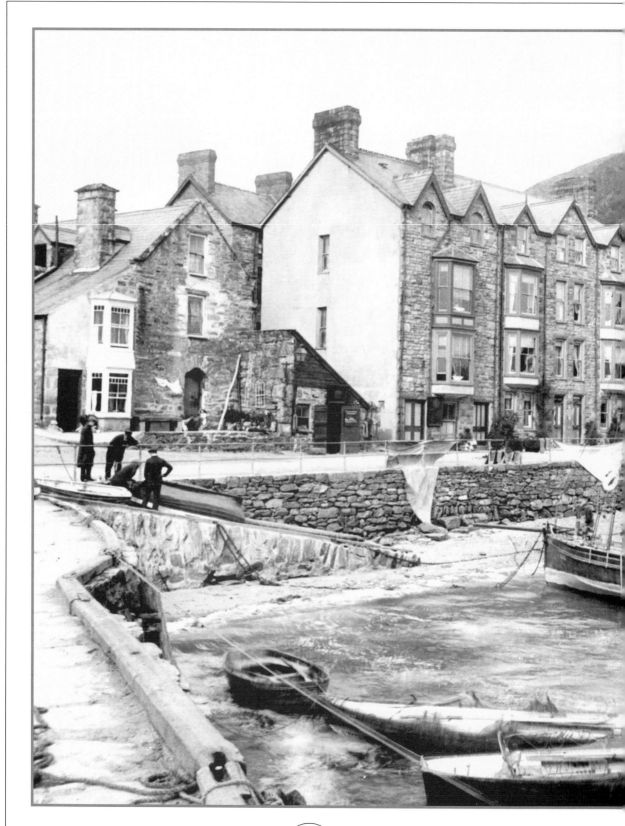

Barmouth, The Harbour 1913 65887
The town was once a shipbuilding centre and the chief port of Merioneth, with a large trade in flannel and knitted stockings. Today, the Three Peaks Race starts here. The quay is still the departure point for the ferry to Fairbourne on the opposite side of the estuary.

▼ **Barmouth, High Street 1908** 60215
This view shows a classic stationer's shop during the Edwardian era.
The display of stock cascades over the frontage - there are local
prints.

▼ **Barmouth, View from the Harbour 1908** 60221
This view looks west from Aberamffra Hill and harbour, just east of
Barmouth. The swing bridge is visible on the left. The harbour itself is
small, and in the late 1890s was managed by a harbour board. Note
the two 4-horse open-top coaches, packed tight with holiday-makers.

▲ **Harlech, The Castle
1889** 21736
Harlech Castle was begun
in 1283. The town
clusters around the
stronghold, clinging to
the steep slopes in a
series of steeply inclined
roads. Harlech Castle is
the very image of a
mediaeval stronghold.
Imposingly set on its crag
overlooking the sands of
Morfa Harlech and the
famous golf course, it is
little changed today from
this view. The song 'Men
of Harlech' relates to its
eight-year siege during
the Wars of the Roses.

◄ **Harlech, High Street 1930** 83614
The narrow ancient streets of Harlech, a town that sprang up to serve the stronghold, have changed little over the years, as is shown by this picture of the High Street. The town was served by a station on the Cambrian railway; as a result, hotels sprang up to cater for the many visitors. The hotel on the right, with its pleasing railings, has a Cyclists' Touring Club sign. The Post Office is down the street to the left.

Harlech, The Castle and the Golf Links 1908 60251
At Harlech, golfers could enjoy the picturesque prospects of the castle and the headland as they walked between holes. The links were created on the Morfa (marsh or sea brink), a tract of well-drained land from which the sea has receded. The greens are well-protected by sand dunes, which in places assume fantastic shapes.

Porthmadog and the Lleyn Peninsula

Extract from Morfa Nefyn 1930 83677

Porthmadog, The Harbour 1908 60719
In this view of the harbour we are looking towards the town clustered on the hillside. The harbour, which was designed specifically for the shipment of slate, opened in 1824, and by 1836 slate arrived here by rail to be loaded onto schooners; we can see schooners moored by the harbourside. The slate arrived at the harbour by rail from Blaenau Ffestiniog, travelling the 13 miles along the narrow gauge Ffestiniog Railway, which now operates as a scenic tourist route. Originally a horse-powered tramway, the Ffestiniog Railway changed to steam power in 1863.

Porthmadog, The Harbour 1908 60718
Formerly the prime harbour for the export of Welsh slate for shipment round the coast, Porthmadog is now a thriving holiday resort. This view of the harbour shows the working quayside and schooners loading slate. Beyond the harbour is the wide sandy estuary of the River Glaslyn, the treacherous Traeth Mawr.

Porthmadog, From Marine Terrace 1899 21807
We are looking over the harbour from Marine Terrace. Several of the port's big fleet of topsail schooners can be seen. These 'western ocean yachts' were built here: they carried slate world-wide, and returned with mixed cargoes. The poet Shelley and his first wife Harriet lived for a while at Tan-yr-allt, near Porthmadog; it was here that a mysterious attempt on his life was said to have been made.

Porthmadog, High Street 1933 85649
This view shows the commercial centre of Pothmadog, with pleasing old Victorian shopfronts to the right. The town was named after its founder, William Madocks (1773-1838), who constructed the harbour in 1821; it is said that he was descended from Prince Madoc, who is thought to have reached America in 1170, 300 years before Columbus. Madocks also developed the small town of Tremadoc on the western side of the Traeth Mawr.

Morfa Bychan, Garreg Wen Lake 1925 77825
Known today for its caravan parks and the long sandy beach of Black Rock sands, Morfa Bychan, just west of Porthmadog, was long celebrated for the story of Dafydd Garreg-Wen, the blind harpist, known for his 'lament', and the hero of Sir Walter Scott's poem 'The Dying Bard'. Here we see the lake and the rocky hill of Moel-y-Gest.

Criccieth, The Golf Club 1913 65789
The golf club was established in 1905, on parkland set high above Cardigan Bay. The landscape in this photograph gives the appearance of great antiquity, with low stone walls and irregularly-shaped fields where sheep graze. Here, the club professional, Mr Owens, is offering instruction at the first hole. Lloyd George was once President of the Club.

◄ **Cricceth and Cardigan
Bay 1931** 84755
This magnificent view was
taken from the east. The
stooks lend period
atmosphere to the harvest
scene; the view today is far
more built-up. Criccieth was
once a modest market town,
but it grew into a select
watering-place when the
Cambrian railway reached it.
Its unspoilt beach, fine
coastal vistas and village
atmosphere drew the more
discerning visitor.

◀ **Criccieth, The Castle 1930** 83630

This resort on the south side of the Llyn peninsula became popular in Victorian times and has remained so ever since. The two sandy beaches are separated by a headland crowned by a Norman castle, developed by Edward I. The statesman Lloyd George (1863-1945) was born in the nearby village of Llanystumdwy, and Criccieth has inevitably become associated with him. The castle was originally a Welsh stronghold fortified by Llewelyn the Great and his sons, but it fell into English hands and was rebuilt in 1285 by Edward I.

▼ **Pwllheli, General View 1891** 29559

Pwllheli (the name means 'saltwater pool') was granted its charter in 1355. Set on the south coast of the Lleyn peninsula, at the mouth of the Penrhos river, it was once a thriving commercial port; but the sea threw a sandbank across the mouth of the Afon Erch, causing the maritime trade to dwindle away. It has since developed as a pleasant seaside resort with a lengthy sandy beach and a little harbour. It is an important market centre.

◀ **Pwllheli, West End Promenade 1898** 42409

This view of the promenade looks south-east around the curving sweep of the bay. The popular 3 ft 6in gauge tramway ran for four miles along this dune-backed coast to Llanbedrog. 'Pwllheli possesses perhaps the finest sandy beach in Wales', says the late Victorian guidebook, 'and the sanitary arrangements are all that could be desired'.

Pwllheli, The Promenade 1898

42286

Horses tread the tramway along Pwllheli's busy promenade at Marian-y-mor (then known as West End). The tramway had opened two years earlier, in 1896, and was closed in 1927. The old town was originally about a quarter of a mile from the sea, but since 1888, a contemporary guidebook tells us, 'the South Beach Land and Building Corporation Limited are building very extensively; and hotels, boarding and private houses are now being erected very rapidly'.

▼ **Pwllheli, The Promenade 1921** 71587
The grand old West End Hotel looks out over the promenade and Cardigan Bay at
Marian-y-mor. The seafront terrace, West End Parade, was built in the late 19th
century. Pwllheli's harbour, with Gimlet Rock at its mouth, had been improved by
the formation of a large embankment to resist encroachment by the sea, and
shipbuilding, fishing and coasting trade went on.

▼ **Pwllheli, The Toll House 1921** 71593
In the days of horse-drawn coaches, this quiet lane would have seen
considerable traffic. The old toll house is at Pont Garreg-Fechan, at the
junction of two former turnpike roads, now the A499 and A497, just
west of Pwllheli. It was already derelict when this picture was taken.

▲ **Abersoch, The Estuary
1894** 34705
From a scattered fishing
village based around two
sandy bays on the
southern coast of the
Lleyn Peninsula,
Abersoch has developed
into a busy resort. There
are superb views from
the sands to Snowdon
and Cadair Idris, and to
the grassy St Tudwal's
Islands just offshore. In
this evocative view,
fishing boats are drawn
up on the slipway onto
the estuary at Abersoch.

◄ **Abersoch, St Tudwal's Hotel 1901** 47009
One of Abersoch's many hostelries, this establishment is now St Tudwal's Inn. St Tudwal (Tugdual) was a Breton, who escaped the fall of Rome in the 6th century and landed on the small islands a little offshore. A ruined chapel is said to be the remains of an oratory he founded. Abersoch was not just a centre for visitors - there were lead mines nearby.

▲ Abersoch, The Congregational Church 1901 47010
Abersoch was keen to advertise itself as 'the Welsh Riviera'. A horse-drawn conveyance is picking up passengers; it is a lovely sunny day, so perhaps they are off for a picnic. The church dates from 1875. Abersoch has grown fast in recent years; it offers a golf course, deep sea fishing, yachting and extensive sands.

◄ Morfa Nefyn 1930 83677
Morfa Nefyn is a holiday village on the Lleyn peninsula; it is situated near Porth Dinllaen on Caernarfon Bay. With barely enough wind to keep under way, small craft lie just offshore.

Snowdon and the Mountains

Extract from Betws-y-Coed
The Llugwy Valley, from above the Miners'
Bridge 1891 29520

Bala, High Street 1896 37706

This spacious town lies at the head of Bala Lake (Llyn Tegid), the largest natural lake in Wales, with a narrow-gauge railway running along its south-eastern shore. It is ringed round by mountains and is now a major watersports centre, though in the 18th century it was renowned for its woollen industry. In Bala's spacious tree-lined High Street we can see the White Lion (centre right) and a pleasing mixture of building styles.

Bala, The White Lion Hotel 1913 65847
Leland wrote that Bala had 'a little poore market' in the 16th century. This vast Victorian hotel, with its half-timbered detail, is a feature of the High Street. Some 60 years earlier George Borrow had stayed here on his tour through 'Wild Wales'; here he drank 'the finest glass of ale he had ever tasted in his life'.

Bala, High Street 1935 86473
Here the street is seemingly deserted in the sunlight, save for a few parked cars; one is waiting outside the Plas Coch Hotel. In the 18th century Bala was a centre for the great religious revival that led to Welsh nonconformism. The town was once known for the manufacture of knitted woollen stockings and gloves, and it is said that George III wore stockings knitted here; much of the knitting was done in the open air.

Bala
The Town and the Lake 1931 84787
This nostalgic and peaceful late-summer view shows corn stooks
above the little town by the lake whose Welsh name, Llyn Tegid,
means 'beautiful lake'. The lake is over three miles long and 100
feet deep; it stretches north-east towards the edges of the town, its
borders wooded and its shores gravelled. Victorian commentators
tell how it abounded with pike, perch, roach and eels.

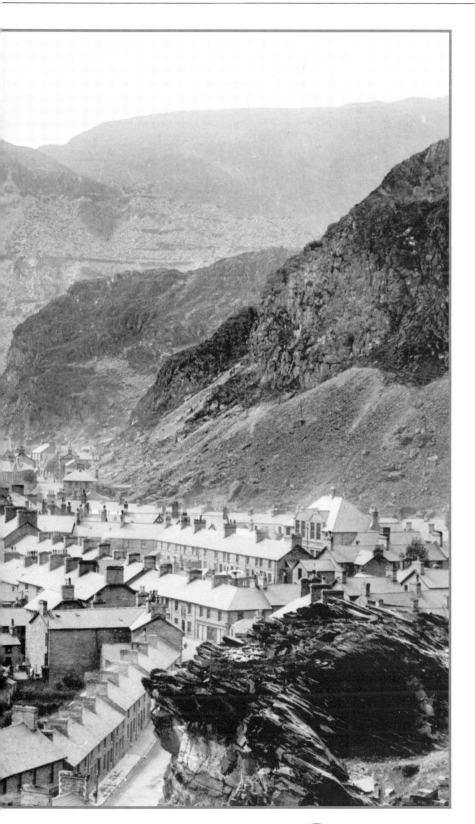

**Blaenau Ffestiniog
General View 1901**
46735
Formerly the slate
capital of Wales, this
slate-grey mountain
town is proud of its
history and happily
promotes its memory.
The quarries, which
roofed Victorian
England from London to
Birmingham and back,
now offer various tours,
and the Ffestiniog
narrow-gauge railway
carries passengers,
rather than slate, to the
coast at Porthmadoc.
This sunlit view looks
across the town
towards the great heaps
of waste from its slate
mines. The railway can
be seen on the left.

◀ **Blaenau Ffestiniog, The Oakley Quarries 1901**
46746
This was one of Blaenau's major quarries; it closed after the Second World War. Ffestiniog slate is of very high quality, and can be split into very thin sheets of great length. It has to be mined because the slate beds dip under a cover of other rocks. The non-slate rocks form huge tips of waste material that scar the hills around, creating a surreal and fantastic landscape.

◄ Blaenau Ffestiniog, Church Street 1901 46741

The awnings are out at the far end of the street to protect the stock in the shop windows from the summer sunshine, and in the foreground we can see frames for the awnings that have not been put up yet. There are several customers for the tobacconist's on the right, and for Alun Jones's shop, a stationers and music sellers, while a horse and cart pauses at the shop on the left.

▼ Blaenau Ffestiniog, General View 1903 49553

This finely-composed study shows the Afon Bowydd, the road bridge, the railway bridge, the ranks of terraces of Blaenau, and the mountains beyond. The town gives the impression of having grown out of the rock that surrounds it - the buildings and their roofs, and the street paving are all formed from the blue-hued slate.

◄ Blaenau Ffestiniog Church Street 1901 46742

This photograph looks uphill towards the great cliff of Carreg Du, which looms over the town's streets. On the right is Owen's butcher's shop, whose hanging meat display would be a health inspector's nightmare. A striped barber's pole projects out over the street, and just beyond it the Temperance Hotel and W J Penny, who sells ales and spirits.

Beddgelert
The Bridge 1889 21832

The small stone village of Beddgelert stands at the confluence of
the Colwyn and Glaslyn rivers. It sits in the shadow of Snowdon,
and is a favourite tourist spot. It is the supposed burial place of
Prince Llewelyn's beloved dog, Gelert, whom he slew in the
mistaken belief that it had killed his son, when in fact the dog had
saved the baby's life. Yet, until about 1800, the village was known
as Beddcelert, the grave of St Celert. The creeper-clad Prince
Llewelyn Hotel is on the right, with two gigs waiting in front of it.
The gracious two-span stone bridge spans the River Colwyn, which
is running low in the summer drought.

Beddgelert, View towards Snowdon 1931 84742A
This magnificent view shows Beddgelert cupped in an encircling ring of mountains. It was described in the late 1890s as 'nestling in a deep romantic vale, engirt by lofty mountains, amidst the grandest scenery in Wales'. It is the perfect site for the ancient priory that once stood here; it was attached to the church of St Celert, and pilgrims have made their way here down the centuries.

Beddgelert, The Village 1933 85667

On the left is Bwthyn Llewelyn (Llewelyn Cottage); its signboard says that it caters for the Cyclists' Touring Club, the National Union and the Clarion Clubs. The cottage was an alehouse prior to the building of the Royal Goat Hotel. It is now a National Trust shop and information centre. Note the old petrol pump on the extreme right.

Beddgelert, The Village 1925 77847

Here we see a conversation piece in the town centre, a century and a quarter after the proprietor of the Royal Goat changed the village's name and erected Gelert's Grave nearby. Walking sticks are displayed outside the shop on the right, and a car draws up outside the Glandwr Café (centre right).

Beddgelert, The Welsh Highland Railway 1925 77842
A train has halted outside the station on the narrow-gauge Welsh Highland Railway. This short-lived railway, which opened in 1922, ran between Porthmadog and Dinas Junction, near Caernarvon, a journey which took two hours. A small section has now been re-opened, and walkers can now walk the abandoned trackway and tunnel.

Snowdon, The Mountain Railway 1897 40059
This 3,650ft-high mountain is the highest in England and Wales. Its Welsh name is Yr Wyddfa, said to mean 'the great burial place'. Today the mountain gives its name to the Snowdonia National Park, playground for outdoor sports enthusiasts. The area has always been hugely popular, ever since the first recorded ascent of Snowdon in 1639 by Thomas Johnson, a botanist.

Snowdon, The Mountain Railway 1896 37764
The crowds came in greater numbers after the Snowdon Mountain Railway opened in 1896, which provided easy access to the summit for hundreds of holidaymakers. The railway is the only rack railway in Britain, and runs for just over four-and-a-half miles from Llanberis to Snowdon Summit. This view shows the brand-new locomotive No 3, 'Wyddra', ascending out of Llanberis towards Snowdon - the rack is clearly visible. The line climbs over 3,000ft, with an average gradient of 1 in 7, although parts of the line are 1 in 5.5. Trains run only in the summer.

◄ **Snowdon, The Summit 1887** 40063
This fine view shows the wooden Snowdon Summit Hotel, with the railway terminus just visible to the left. The wooden structure we see in this picture was replaced in 1936. From the summit there are magnificent and extensive views. There are several viaducts on the railway; one is 500ft long, and has 14 arches each with a 30ft span.

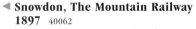

Snowdon, The Mountain Railway 1897 40062

Here we see a train nearing the summit at Snowdon. One of the Swiss-built steam locomotives propels the standard single coach up the final leg; the railway starts near the Victoria Hotel, 350ft above sea level, and there are four intermediate stations before the summit is reached. A return trip takes some two hours. Snowdon consists of four rugged and precipitous ridges separated by 100ft-deep hollows, and is formed of slate and porphyry.

Betws-y-Coed, The Llugwy Valley 1891 29520

This famous resort on the Holyhead road, in the narrow, deeply-glaciated valley of the river Conwy, became popular when it was reached by the railway in Victorian times. It has remained a tourist honeypot ever since. There are several fine Victorian hotels from which visitors can still explore the fine landscape and foaming rivers. This evocative view of the deep and leafy valley was taken from above the famous Miners' Bridge.

Betws-y-Coed, The Miners' Bridge c1955 B79185

This wooden bridge lies on the line of the Roman road, Sarn Helen. A popular destination of walkers, it was built to allow the miners of Pentre Du to reach the mines in the hills; a mile west of Betws-y-Coed, paths lead through the meadows to this steeply-inclined gangway across the river.

Betws-y-Coed, The Royal Oak Hotel 1892 30094
The artist David Cox painted the original signboard of this old coaching inn when, with several fellow artists, he frequented Betws in the first half of the 19th century, painting the Machno Falls. It was popular in Victorian times as a centre for fishing and riding, and for trekking among the mountains and waterfalls. Today a visitor centre in the stables tells of Snowdonia National Park's natural history and that of Gwydir Forest.

Capel Curig, Llugwy Valley 1891 29537
This little hamlet lies on the River Llugwy, at the foot of Snowdon. It is now home to the National Mountaineering Centre at Plas Brenin, but has been known for many years for its superb view of the Snowdon 'horseshoe'. This photograph shows the wooded valley at Capel Curig. In the Victorian era it was very popular with anglers, and there were coaches carrying visitors from Betws-y-Coed to Bangor and Llanberis.

Bethesda, The Town c1955 B77016
This Snowdonian village on the Holyhead Road (A5) lies at the mouth of the pass of Nant Ffrancon, beneath the famous Penrhyn slate quarries, once the largest in the world and still producing slate today. It developed as a slate mining town for the thousands of workers once employed at Penrhyn, but it took its name from the large chapel in the middle of town. Here we are looking across the town towards the mountain, Y Garn, and the Penrhyn quarries. St Ann's Church, built in 1865, is on the right. The Penrhyn quarries are 1,140 ft deep.

Bethesda, Penrhyn Quarry Engine c1955 B77025
This engine is the 'Sybil Mary'. A tram road was constructed by Lord Penrhyn in 1872 to link the Penrhyn quarries and the new harbour at Port Penrhyn near Bangor.

Caernarvon and Anglesey

*Extract from Beaumaris
The Pier 1911* 63294

Caernarvon, The Castle 1891 29499
Known today for its massive castle, one of Edward
I's chain of fortresses built to subdue the Welsh, this
town on the shore of the Menai Strait at the mouth
of the River Seiont is now staunchly Welsh-
speaking. It was formerly an important harbour,
shipping a variety of goods. It is an ancient place,
originally Segontium, a Roman fortress constructed
in AD 78. The massive castle, begun in 1285,
remains unchanged since this picture was taken. In
contrast, the shipping in the harbour has changed
dramatically. Here, schooners, including the
'Catherine' in the foreground, lie alongside the slate
quay, waiting to be loaded with Snowdon slate for
transportation to Europe.

◀ **Caernarvon, The Square 1933** 85673
In this view of the square, coaches are parked in the broad open expanse. The town consists of ten streets within the walls, which are defended by round towers, and around twenty outside. It is the capital of the county, and in the late 1890s held assizes and sessions, and was the militia headquarters.

◀ Caernarvon, The Castle and Swing Bridge 1906 54832

Here we see the harbour swing bridge, with the important Slate Quay visible on the right. This was connected to the slate mines by a narrow gauge railway. The harbour pier and landing-slip could accept vessels up to 400 tons. Over 200 vessels were registered to the town in 1893.

▼ Caernarvon, Castle Square 1906 54825

Dominating Castle Square ('Y Maes' in Welsh) at the west end of the town stands the great bulk of the castle. The structure covers two and a half acres and is in the shape of an irregular oblong. There are 13 massive towers in pentagonal, hexagonal and octagonal designs.

◀ Bangor, St Deniol's Cathedral 1906 54822

The first monastic settlement was founded here by St Deniol in AD525, some 70 years before St Augustine arrived in Canterbury. The site was much fought over by the Vikings, the Normans and the Welsh, so that the cathedral has been rebuilt on several occasions. The cathedral is modest in size and squats in a hollow. The nave with its six arches and the western tower were built in the early years of the 16th century. It was restored by Gilbert Scott between 1866 and 1875.

Bangor, High Street and the Clock 1908

60734

Looking across the Menai Straits to Anglesey, the city of Bangor is the largest town in the north-west corner of Wales, the former principality of Gwynedd, and home to an ancient diocese and the University College of North Wales. The cathedral has been a site of Christian worship for longer than that at Canterbury. Horse-drawn vehicles ply the High Street on a summer morning; a sign on the clock tower directs visitors to the sea-water baths and the pier. Note the poster for Rose's lime juice, right. The view is very different today, since the building behind the red-brick clock tower has been demolished and the site redeveloped.

▼ **Penrhyn Castle, From the Park 1870** 1629B
The magnificent early 19th-century mock-Norman castle is shown
here photographed from the park. It was built by the Pennant family
on the proceeds of their huge Penrhyn slate quarries at Bethesda.

▼ **Bangor, Garth from the Ferry 1890** 23180
This view was taken from the ferry. It looks southwards towards the Garth and
Bangor, which is backed by the Snowdon mountains. Bangor's chief trade was the
export of slates, mined from Lord Penrhyn's quarries at Bethesda, and carried by
rail to Port Penrhyn. The quay here was 300 yards long.

▲ **Bangor, High Street
1908** 60732
Bangor's main street runs
between the station and
the harbour. It is shown
here crowded with
shoppers and an early
car. The street today has
been partly
pedestrianised. In the
early years of the 19th
century, there were only
93 houses in the town.
However, after the
construction of the
bridges over the Straits
and the opening of the
railway, Bangor grew at a
fast rate into a thriving
holiday town.

◀ **Bangor, The Pier 1897**
40045
The Victorian pier was built in 1896 and juts out 1,500 feet into the turbulent waters of the Menai Strait, stretching two-thirds of the distance to Anglesey. It is pictured here with Snowdonia in the background. It was refurbished in the 1980s.

Bangor, The Pier 1911 63312
This splendid view of the pier, which had charming little kiosks
along its entire length, shows a paddle steamer approaching the
landing stage. The town was part of a regular route from Liverpool,
with steamers taking on passengers at Llandudno and Beaumaris.

Menai, The Suspension Bridge 1891 29485
The elegant suspension bridge, built over the Menai Strait
by Thomas Telford as part of his Holyhead Road, gave its
name to the little town on the northern side of the
narrow strait, between the island of Anglesey and
mainland North Wales.

The Menai Suspension Bridge 1890 23187
We are looking from Anglesey to the mainland along the 579ft-long suspension bridge. The bridge was the first structure of its kind in the world, and is pictured here when it was 64 years old. The bridge is best viewed from Belgian Promenade which overlooks the water. This is a view from Anglesey across the strait. Rip tides up and down the strait made the ferry a dangerous option, and earned the Menai the nickname 'the British Bosphorus'.

◀ **Beaumaris, The Pier 1911** 63294
Beaumaris means 'beautiful marsh'. From mediaeval times until the 19th century, Beaumaris was Anglesey's main harbour; 111 sailing vessels and 8 steamers were registered in 1893. Copper ores, slate and marble were exported. Here a paddle steamer approaches the pier, one of many vessels plying the coastal waters between Bangor and Liverpool.

Beaumaris, The West End 1904 53029

One of Anglesey's best-known sailing resorts, at the eastern end of the Menai Strait, Beaumaris was founded by Edward I, who built one of his great castles here, although it was never finished. In this view, two old salts and a boy look out across the pier and the Menai Strait to the mountains of Snowdonia. Beaumaris was popular with tourists: it offered fine bathing grounds, pleasant walks and a ferry to Bangor.

▼ Beaumaris, Castle Street 1911
63300

The town, granted its charter by Edward I in 1294, still has something of an English air, and much fine architecture. Castle Street is one of the two main streets, the other being Watergate. The town developed fast in Victorian times, and in 1896 had a commodious town hall, assembly rooms, a custom house, a literary institute, a club, a market-house and a free grammar school. Picture postcards, hugely popular at the time, are for sale on the left - perhaps they included Frith postcards.

◄ Beaumaris, Castle Street 1933 85721

This view of Castle Street was taken in the summer sunlight, with a couple of parked cars and a few pedestrians. The Old Bull's Head is on the left: this famous hostelry was originally built in 1472, and was rebuilt in 1617. Both Dr Johnson and Charles Dickens stayed here.

Holyhead
The South Stack Lighthouse 1892 30299
Holyhead is best known as the ferry port for Ireland, and stands on Holy
Island, linked by a causeway to the Isle of Anglesey. It is the point of
destination of Telford's most famous road, now the A5, built rapid
communication between London and Dublin. Holyhead has a long tradition
of seafaring: the remains of a possible Roman naval base lie next to St Cybi's
church. The rocky islet is joined to Holy Island by a footbridge at the bottom
of a zigzag path. The lighthouse was built in 1809; its keepers left for the last
time in 1985, when it was automated. The ancient folded rock cliffs are a
superb breeding site for seabirds.

Holyhead, Market Street c1955 H105126
Like any seaport town, Holyhead is cosmopolitan, noisy and busy, as shown by this picture of Market Street with its fine array of shops. It has been the main port for Ireland since the early 19th century. Its local industries of shipbuilding and ropemaking gained new life after the building of a new, deeper 2,000 foot-long harbour in 1880. Before this, packet steamers were unable to land passengers.

◄ **Llanfairfechan, Main Street 1908** 60771
This pleasant stone-built Victorian seaside resort, just west of Conwy, clusters beneath the steep craggy slopes of the coastal mountains on Conwy Bay. It is now bypassed by the A55, and looks across the broad eastern approaches of the Menai Strait to Anglesey. The Frith photograph shows the narrow twisting Main Street constrained beneath the mountain. The few pedestrians and single horse-drawn cart give no hint that this spot was soon to become a major traffic bottleneck.

Conway and the Holiday Coast

Extract from Rhyl, The Beach 1913 65731

◀ **Llanfairfechan, The Sands 1890**
23212
The resort is described in an 1890s guidebook: 'it has a wooded and well-sheltered situation and a singularly lovely seaward prospect. No great crowds of holiday-makers are seen in our illustration, but the astute observer may discern significant signs of the rising watering-place'.

Penmaenmawr
The Parade 1913 65677
Today, Penmaenmawr is a small, much-loved seaside resort
overlooking Conwy Bay and backed by precipitous coastal
mountains. However, in earlier times it was the terror of travellers
on the Holyhead Road. This stretch of the coast road was merely a
ledge cut along the crumbly cliffs, and was notorious for accidents.
Penmaenmawr was originally a port for the shipment of local stone;
it became the favourite holiday resort of W M Gladstone, who
always spoke with affection of 'dear old Penmaenmawr'.

Conway
The Castle c1865 5161

Set at the mouth of the River Conway, or Conwy, this mediaeval
walled town with its famous castle, one of Edward I's 'iron ring'
around Wales, is still remarkably self-contained. The new A55 road
tunnel beneath the river diverts through-traffic from its streets. The
quay is busy today with pleasure craft, rather than the commercial
traffic of the past. This early photograph shows Conway Castle and
Telford's graceful suspension bridge of 1826, with Stephenson's
tubular railway bridge of 1848 just behind it. Today the road bridge
of 1958 blocks the view of the earlier bridges.

Conway, The Castle and the Bridges 1906 54812

Conwy was once an important port with a major fishing fleet. There are mussel beds at the mouth of the river, while freshwater oysters found upstream have been famous for their pearls. Telford's 1826 bridge measures 327 ft long. It hangs on eight chains in two sets over two piers, with adjustment at one end into the rock under the castle, and at the other end into solid rock. It was built for his Holyhead road and replaced a notorious ferry across the dangerous waters of the Conwy estuary.

Conway, The Castle and the Suspension Bridge 1906 54810

We can see a tower of Stephenson's 412ft-long tubular railway bridge in the centre of the picture. This structure was built on the line of the old L & NWR Railway in 1848. A 19th-century guide describes how it increases in height above high water from around 22 feet at the ends to 25 feet at the centre. The two tubes are each 14 feet wide and weigh around 1,300 tons.

Llandudno, The Promenade 1890 23236
Here we see Llandudno's spacious, sweeping promenade in its heyday, looking towards the massive limestone headland of the Great Orme, yet to be cumbered with its famous tramway and cable car. Commerce was kept away from the front and its grandiose hotels to preserve its genteel atmosphere - on the right we can see the Adelphi Hotel and the Imperial Hotel.

Llandudno, Gloddaeth Street 1890 23247
As late as 1840 Llandudno was little more than a small village, frequented by a few stalwart visitors. Here we see a charming view of two donkey carts standing at the foot of Upper Madoc Street (now Arvon Avenue) with buildings stretching out far beyond to the rugged hills. The Presbyterian church is on the left and the spire of the United Reformed Church on the right.

**Llandudno, The
Promenade 1898**

41487

'The Queen of Welsh
resorts', Llandudno
preserves much of its
Victorian flavour, with
its sweeping
promenade faced by
numerous hotels, its
expanse of sands
between the headlands
of the Great and Little
Ormes, its pier, its wide
streets and its shops
beneath glass canopies
supported by delicately
decorated cast-iron
pillars. This view looks
towards the Great
Orme, the Grand Hotel,
the pier and the huge
pier pavilion - later
destroyed by fire -
which seated 2,000.
Bathing machines can
be seen on the beach.
A late 19th-century
guide sings Llandudno's
praises: 'the bright blue
waters of the sea, the
majestic ruins and
bridges of Conway, all
combine to form a
prospect of wondrous
beauty, which, bounded
by the undulating
outlines of the
mountains, is well worth
a pilgrimage to
contemplate'.

▼ **Llandudno, The Pier 1890** 23249
Pictured here with promenaders protected from the sun by parasols, the pier
was built in 1875. The 1,400 ft-long structure, tucked beneath the cliffs of the
Great Orme, gives excellent views back to the promenade and its hotels. The
landing stage was built for steamers to Liverpool and Holyhead.

▼ **Llandudno, Happy Valley 1913** 65712
Visitors enjoy the broad prospects from the pleasure gardens on the Great Orme.
Today, the cable car mounts the giant promontory of the Great Orme to the
Summit Hotel through the centre of the picture; the only way up used to be a
tramway, built in 1903. Crowds in summer flocked to attend the open-air services
at the tiny church of St Tudno on the summit.

▲ **Llandudno, Mostyn
Street 1890** 23246
Mostyn Street is one of
Llandudno's main
shopping streets; we see
it here pictured in bright
sunlight. There are plenty
of horse-drawn
conveyances, while some
of the awnings and cast-
iron canopies that are
such a picturesque
feature today are visible
on the right. The
Birmingham Arms and
Dining Rooms proclaims
itself with a prominent
signboard.

◄ **Rhos-on-Sea, The Seafront 1921** 70794
This seaside resort and residential haven developed from the 1860s. Despite being continuous with Colwyn Bay, it preserves its own peaceful character. Its real name is Llandrillo-yn-Rhos, and the minute 6th-century St Trillo's chapel, built over a holy well, still stands on the promenade. On the right can be seen the landward section of the Victorian pier, which was demolished in 1954. The pier was acquired from Douglas in the Isle of Man in 1895, and was erected here in a bid to attract more tourists. Its place is now taken by a breakwater.

Colwyn Bay, The Beach 1898 42375
This popular seaside resort sits in a wide sweep of bay on the north coast, with wooded hills behind the promenade, which fronts miles of safe sandy beach. The resort, less brash than Rhyl and its cohorts, has been well patronised since the 1860s, and prides itself on its mild climate. Wonderfully evocative of a real seaside holiday, this picture shows all age-groups enjoying themselves on the famous Colwyn Bay sands, where the pier was soon to stand. The building on the right, with its steeply-pitched slate roof, is the old Colwyn Bay Hotel, demolished in 1975. Note the pram with its penny-farthing-style wheels.

Colwyn Bay, The Pier 1900 46265

The pier is pictured with its grand pavilion, during the year it opened. Well-dressed 'promenaders' stroll along the parade, while in the foreground a troupe of minstrels entertain a crowd of holidaymakers. A late Victorian guide book noted that 'of the fine climate of Colwyn Bay there can be no doubt. Flowers bloom here until well on towards Christmas, and are out again in some profusion in February'.

Colwyn Bay, West Promenade 1906 54784

The beach runs in a glorious sweep around the bay. The sands slope gently, offering safe bathing for children, and extend for a mile and more. It was observed in the 1890s that 'the deep water, wherein the expert swimmer loves to disport himself, is not too far out to be tiresome'. The curving promenade is three miles long, running westwards from Rhos on Sea to Old Colwyn. The house on the extreme left offers lodgings to let.

Colwyn Bay, The Pier Pavillion 1900 46268
Crowds stroll along the pier, beside the original Pier Pavilion, which is advertising the popular French conductor Jules Rivieres and his grand orchestra. The pavilion, which seated 2,500 people, was destroyed by fire, as was its successor. Restoration of the by then derelict pier began in 1996. The elegance of the pier was reflected in the broad streets of the town, which were built to resemble fine boulevards.

Old Colwyn, A Street Scene 1906 54796
Prior to the development of the coastal resort at Colwyn Bay in Victorian times, the old village, lying to the east and just inland from the coast, was known merely as Colwyn. It is still an important shopping centre. This view is still recognisable today, although there have been many changes over the years. The tower of St John the Baptist's church in Station Road is visible on the left.

▼ Abergele, Market Street 1890 23331

This pleasant market town lies just inland from the chalets and caravans of the 'honky-tonk' north coast between Rhyl and Colwyn Bay. It is close to quiet wooded hills, and to Gwyrch Castle, a battlemented mock castle built in the early 19th century. This street is so free from traffic that a dog can sun himself in the roadway. Note the bolts of fabric outside D G Roberts & Co, 'Drapers, Silk Mercers, Hatters, established 1842'.

▼ Abergele, Market Street c1965 A10033

Barclays Bank, which has by now replaced part of the terrace on the left, dates from 1924: it is a typical example of the pretentious architecture beloved of banks. Regardless of the unsympathetic way it clashes with the rest of the street, the bank goes all out to impress. The timber-framed building on the right was built in 1906 as a temperance club. The spire of the former town hall, built in 1867, is a recognisable landmark. Market day was Saturday in Victorian times.

▲ Abergele, Market Street 1895 36573
Only 5 years after photograph No 23331, D G Roberts have expanded: their shopfront is longer and fronted by a mini-arcade, and they now have a first-floor showroom with a plate-glass window. The town consists of this single wide street, running about a mile from the shore. Tradesmen's carts are much in evidence in this view. Although there are several changes to the street, the town hall is still a landmark.

◄ **Abergele, The River Gele 1890** 23336
This unidentified ford is possibly located where the A55 expressway now passes the town. The water level seems very low, luckily for the lady with the long skirts.

Rhyl, Donkeys on the Sands 1891 29151
Donkeys are awaiting the arrival of the day's holidaymakers on the beach. A fisherwoman in a tall hat stands behind the donkey boys and their mounts. The Victoria Pier behind them cost £23,000 to build in 1867; in 1891 a grand pavilion was built at the entrance, capable of seating 2,500 people, and one of the largest organs in Britain was installed behind the stage. Rhyl Sands are famous as a great windy expanse of beach facing into Liverpool Bay. They were painted with vigour by David Cox in 1854, and were the inspiration in the 1870s for Gerard Manley Hopkins's poem 'The Sea and the Skylark'.

▼ Rhyl, The Pavilion and Victoria Pier c1867 2254

The seafront itself is a noisy bustle of amusements, and has been for generations, providing seaside fun for the many. This early picture was probably taken to mark the pier's opening in 1867, a time when the possession of such a structure was indispensable to a seaside resort. A poster on the pier pavilion proclaims that 'Chris Reynolds and his Splendid Band' are playing tonight. The pier was demolished in 1972.

▼ Rhyl, The Queen's Palace 1903 49540

The Queen's Palace, attached to the Queen's Hotel, is pictured the year after it opened. The precursor of Rhyl's amusement arcades, it advertised '... theatre, ballroom, restaurant, waxworks, winter garden, underground canal with gondolas, arcade of shops, zoo, sideshows, all provided on a lavish scale with every modern refinement ...' In this photograph, the posters on the front of the building tell us that this week we will be entertained by Ernie Myers, Lily Lonsdale, Fred Carey, Los Gopanos, Blanche Gerard and Marie Reeves; admission is 1s.

▲ Rhyl, The Beach 1913
65731
This bustling scene looks east to the pier pavilion and the pier. The bucket and spades, bare feet, donkeys and wickerwork basket chairs recapture a vanished era. 'The sands form an excellent bathing-ground, entirely free from danger', says a Victorian guidebook. 'Hence Rhyl has become noted for the number of children that visit it, and these little ones find an inexhaustible fund of pleasure on its beach'.

◄ **Rhyl, The Parade 1900** 46284
Backed by the tall 52-year-old buildings of the Esplanade, the Parade was Rhyl's only real attempt at elegant seaside architecture. The two-mile-long parade overlooks the sandy beach; at the west end an extensive area was laid out as winter gardens. A pavilion for concerts and other entertainments had been built in 1891 in the form of a Maltese cross. There were numerous hotels in the town, and two hydropathic establishments; 'there are several convalescent hospitals', says a contemporary gazetteer, adding rather ominously 'and a cemetery'.

Rhyl, The Promenade 1913 65725
This photograph shows the crowded Promenade the year before the outbreak of war, and looks west to the pier pavilion and the tall buildings of the esplanade. West of the pier a marine lake for pleasure boating was formed in 1895; it had nearly 40 acres of water and a 3-acre island. Today the 240ft skytower dominates the seafront, and offers stunning views along the coast and up the vale of Clwyd.

Prestatyn, High Street 1895 36600
Prestatyn is a very popular holiday resort, with three beaches and major leisure facilities. Its development from a little village straggling up a single high street began in 1870. However, it has an ancient lineage, and the Romans established a major settlement nearby. This view looks down Prestatyn's High Street, towards the new Rehoboth Welsh Presbyterian Chapel, which had opened the previous year, and the spire of Christ Church, built in 1863.

Prestatyn, High Street 1895 36602

Prestatyn's station on the Chester and Holyhead section of the L & NWR meant that it became increasingly popular with holidaymakers, especially with those from the Liverpool area. This charming study shows the lower part of the High Street on a breezy summer's day. Shopkeepers stand at their doors at the little parade of shops; prams are parked outside, and a boy gazes longingly at the display of hoops.

Prestatyn, A Street Scene 1895 36603

In the 18th century, Prestatyn was a centre for the lead-mining districts of north-east Wales. Before that, it was the site of a castle built before the time of Henry II and held by the Prince of Powys, Owain Cyfeiliog. This view shows Prestatyn's position at the foot of the majestic Clwydian Hills. Today it is known as the start or finish of the 152-mile-long Offa's Dyke National Trail.

Wrexham and the East

Extract from Wrexham
High Street 1895 36282

St Asaph, Elwy Bridge 1890 23293
This tiny cathedral city stands above the confluence
of the River Clwyd and its tributary the Elwy. The
cathedral is the smallest in Britain. St Asaph, named
after its second bishop, may have been the site of
Roman Varis, but the present town was founded in
Saxon times. During the 17th century, Bishop
William Morgan translated the Bible into Welsh. This
view across the 18th-century bridge looks past the
gate to the Bishop's palace and up to the cathedral.
Apart from a petrol station on the right and an
increase in traffic, the scene is virtually unchanged
today.

Denbigh, Market Place 1888 20848
This pleasant stone-built market town, on the western side of the lovely vale of Clwyd, climbs the hillside crowned by its ruinous castle. Still recognisable today, this view shows on the right the well-known arcade of shops which started life as an island block between Back Row and the present Market Place; note the rabbits hanging outside the butcher's on the right. In the background is the Star Corn Warehouse.

◀ **Berwyn, The Chain Bridge Hotel 1888** 20681
Berwyn is a lonely spot west of Llangollen, where the half-timbered Chain Bridge Hotel and the station on the old Llangollen-Corwen railway stand beside the River Dee as it enters a small gorge. Here the railway, canal and Holyhead Road (A5) run beside the river amid the Berwyn Mountains, a wild heather-clad upland. King's Bridge spans the river on the left of the picture.

Denbigh, The Castle 1888
20854

Here we see Victorian children at play in a playground within the castle ruins. The castle, which dates from 1282, was left to slide into decay following its siege during the Civil War in 1645. It held out for the king, and was thereafter slighted by Cromwell's men. The journalist-cum-explorer Henry Morton Stanley was born John Rowlands in a cottage beneath the castle.

Mold, The Town Centre c1950 M201036

This old market town in the hills between the Cheshire Plain and the vale of Clwyd became the county town for the 1974 county of Clwyd. The Welsh name, Yr Wyddgrug, means 'the mound'. Richard Wilson, the landscape painter, and Daniel Own, 'the Welsh Dickens', are buried at Mold. This view shows the main crossroads at the centre of town, looking up High Street towards St Mary's church. The building in the centre left is the Market Hall of 1850; the Assembly Room in the third storey was added later in the century. A market is still held at the lower end of High Street.

Hawarden, The Village 1903
49656

A border town with a ruinous castle built by Henry III, Hawarden lies close to Chester on the former main road into Wales from the Dee lowlands and the Cheshire Plain. The A55 has now bypassed the town. The present Hawarden Castle, Broadlane Hall, is a castellated affair which was for many years home to W M Gladstone, whose wife had inherited it. This view of the road junction at the village centre shows the ornate drinking fountain erected to commemorate the golden wedding of Mr and Mrs Gladstone in 1889.

Hawarden, The House of Correction c1900 H43302
Here the old village lock-up is pictured with two boys. The building, whose simple Doric doorcase we see here, stands near the council offices at the end of Glynne Way, and dates from the 1740s.

Chirk, The Castle c1955 C366777

A small town at the gateway to Wales, close to the English border and Offa's Dyke, Chirk is noted both for its castle, in continuous occupation from the 13th century, and its position at the entrance to the beautiful Glyn Ceirog, for many years an important route into mid Wales. The present castle dates from the 14th century; it was bought in 1595 by Sir Thomas Myddleton, who installed its beautiful but incongruous windows.

Chirk, Ceirog Valley c1955 C366022

A little beyond the 450yd-long tunnel at Chirk, the Llangollen Canal is suddenly carried 70 feet in the air over this spectacular stone aqueduct. Here we are looking north across the valley, along Telford's 70ft-high aqueduct of 1801, which carries the Ellesmere Canal. Hugging it closely all the way is the 100 ft-high viaduct, built in 1848 to carry the Shrewsbury and Chester Railway.

Wrexham, High Street 1895 36282 Wrexham stands on a tributary of the river Dee. It has a long history - it was known to the Saxons as Wrightesham or Wrightelesham. Elihu Yale, founder of Yale University in the USA, came from the Wrexham area (his family was associated with Erddig Hall), and he is buried at St Giles's church. The town developed fast during the 19th century, and became an important centre for brick and tile manufacture. Brewing was also an important industry in the town: a brewer's cart is standing outside a public house on the left.

Wrexham, High Street 1903 49688
Wrexham 'comprises several spacious, well-paved streets', says a contemporary gazetteer, 'and has undergone great improvement by reconstruction of buildings and the construction of new streets'. Wrexham's prosperity was founded on its position at the centre of the north Welsh coalfield, which fed local iron-, steel- and gasworks. Here we can see shopkeepers and many of their potential customers posing for the camera outside the shops.

Wrexham, Hope Street and the Talbot Inn 1895 36284
The Talbot Inn is on the right of this view. Mr Holt the landlord offers his customers locally-brewed Wrexham Ales.
The town was a centre for brewing, malting, tanning and mining as well as staging Monday, Thursday and
Saturday markets. There was a market-hall, free library, reading room, art school and an infirmary.

Wrexham, Hope Street 1903 49689
This view looks towards St Giles's church. It was built in 1472, and its 140ft-high tower, richly decorated with
sculptured ornamentation, is traditionally listed as one of the 'seven wonders of Wales'. The church contains
several interesting monuments, including one by Roubilliac. In this photograph we can see Victorian shop fronts in
a range of styles, a glimpse of a world that time has swept away.

Index

Frith Book Co Titles

www.francisfrith.co.uk

The Frith Book Company publishes over 100 new titles each year. A selection of those currently available are listed below. For latest catalogue please contact Frith Book Co.
Town Books 96 pages, approximately 100 photos. *County and Themed Books* 128 pages, approximately 150 photos (unless specified). All titles hardback with laminated case and jacket, except those indicated pb (paperback)

Amersham, Chesham & Rickmansworth (pb)	1-85937-340-2	£9.99	Devon (pb)	1-85937-297-x	£9.99
Andover (pb)	1-85937-292-9	£9.99	Devon Churches (pb)	1-85937-250-3	£9.99
Aylesbury (pb)	1-85937-227-9	£9.99	Dorchester (pb)	1-85937-307-0	£9.99
Barnstaple (pb)	1-85937-300-3	£9.99	Dorset (pb)	1-85937-269-4	£9.99
Basildon Living Memories (pb)	1-85937-515-4	£9.99	Dorset Coast (pb)	1-85937-299-6	£9.99
Bath (pb)	1-85937-419-0	£9.99	Dorset Living Memories (pb)	1-85937-584-7	£9.99
Bedford (pb)	1-85937-205-8	£9.99	Down the Severn (pb)	1-85937-560-x	£9.99
Bedfordshire Living Memories	1-85937-513-8	£14.99	Down The Thames (pb)	1-85937-278-3	£9.99
Belfast (pb)	1-85937-303-8	£9.99	Down the Trent	1-85937-311-9	£14.99
Berkshire (pb)	1-85937-191-4	£9.99	East Anglia (pb)	1-85937-265-1	£9.99
Berkshire Churches	1-85937-170-1	£17.99	East Grinstead (pb)	1-85937-138-8	£9.99
Berkshire Living Memories	1-85937-332-1	£14.99	East London	1-85937-080-2	£14.99
Black Country	1-85937-497-2	£12.99	East Sussex (pb)	1-85937-606-1	£9.99
Blackpool (pb)	1-85937-393-3	£9.99	Eastbourne (pb)	1-85937-399-2	£9.99
Bognor Regis (pb)	1-85937-431-x	£9.99	Edinburgh (pb)	1-85937-193-0	£8.99
Bournemouth (pb)	1-85937-545-6	£9.99	England In The 1880s	1-85937-331-3	£17.99
Bradford (pb)	1-85937-204-x	£9.99	Essex - Second Selection	1-85937-456-5	£14.99
Bridgend (pb)	1-85937-386-0	£7.99	Essex (pb)	1-85937-270-8	£9.99
Bridgwater (pb)	1-85937-305-4	£9.99	Essex Coast	1-85937-342-9	£14.99
Bridport (pb)	1-85937-327-5	£9.99	Essex Living Memories	1-85937-490-5	£14.99
Brighton (pb)	1-85937-192-2	£8.99	Exeter	1-85937-539-1	£9.99
Bristol (pb)	1-85937-264-3	£9.99	Exmoor (pb)	1-85937-608-8	£9.99
British Life A Century Ago (pb)	1-85937-213-9	£9.99	Falmouth (pb)	1-85937-594-4	£9.99
Buckinghamshire (pb)	1-85937-200-7	£9.99	Folkestone (pb)	1-85937-124-8	£9.99
Camberley (pb)	1-85937-222-8	£9.99	Frome (pb)	1-85937-317-8	£9.99
Cambridge (pb)	1-85937-422-0	£9.99	Glamorgan	1-85937-488-3	£14.99
Cambridgeshire (pb)	1-85937-420-4	£9.99	Glasgow (pb)	1-85937-190-6	£9.99
Cambridgeshire Villages	1-85937-523-5	£14.99	Glastonbury (pb)	1-85937-338-0	£7.99
Canals And Waterways (pb)	1-85937-291-0	£9.99	Gloucester (pb)	1-85937-232-5	£9.99
Canterbury Cathedral (pb)	1-85937-179-5	£9.99	Gloucestershire (pb)	1-85937-561-8	£9.99
Cardiff (pb)	1-85937-093-4	£9.99	Great Yarmouth (pb)	1-85937-426-3	£9.99
Carmarthenshire (pb)	1-85937-604-5	£9.99	Greater Manchester (pb)	1-85937-266-x	£9.99
Chelmsford (pb)	1-85937-310-0	£9.99	Guildford (pb)	1-85937-410-7	£9.99
Cheltenham (pb)	1-85937-095-0	£9.99	Hampshire (pb)	1-85937-279-1	£9.99
Cheshire (pb)	1-85937-271-6	£9.99	Harrogate (pb)	1-85937-423-9	£9.99
Chester (pb)	1-85937-382 8	£9.99	Hastings and Bexhill (pb)	1-85937-131-0	£9.99
Chesterfield (pb)	1-85937-378-x	£9.99	Heart of Lancashire (pb)	1-85937-197-3	£9.99
Chichester (pb)	1-85937-228-7	£9.99	Helston (pb)	1-85937-214-7	£9.99
Churches of East Cornwall (pb)	1-85937-249-x	£9.99	Hereford (pb)	1-85937-175-2	£9.99
Churches of Hampshire (pb)	1-85937-207-4	£9.99	Herefordshire (pb)	1-85937-567-7	£9.99
Cinque Ports & Two Ancient Towns	1-85937-492-1	£14.99	Herefordshire Living Memories	1-85937-514-6	£14.99
Colchester (pb)	1-85937-188-4	£8.99	Hertfordshire (pb)	1-85937-247-3	£9.99
Cornwall (pb)	1-85937-229-5	£9.99	Horsham (pb)	1-85937-432-8	£9.99
Cornwall Living Memories	1-85937-248-1	£14.99	Humberside (pb)	1-85937-605-3	£9.99
Cotswolds (pb)	1-85937-230-9	£9.99	Hythe, Romney Marsh, Ashford (pb)	1-85937-256-2	£9.99
Cotswolds Living Memories	1-85937-255-4	£14.99	Ipswich (pb)	1-85937-424-7	£9.99
County Durham (pb)	1-85937-398-4	£9.99	Isle of Man (pb)	1-85937-268-6	£9.99
Croydon Living Memories (pb)	1-85937-162-0	£9.99	Isle of Wight (pb)	1-85937-429-8	£9.99
Cumbria (pb)	1-85937-621-5	£9.99	Isle of Wight Living Memories	1-85937-304-6	£14.99
Derby (pb)	1-85937-367-4	£9.99	Kent (pb)	1-85937-189-2	£9.99
Derbyshire (pb)	1-85937-196-5	£9.99	Kent Living Memories(pb)	1-85937-401-8	£9.99
Derbyshire Living Memories	1-85937-330-5	£14.99	Kings Lynn (pb)	1-85937-334-8	£9.99

Available from your local bookshop or from the publisher

Frith Book Co Titles (continued)

Title	ISBN	Price	Title	ISBN	Price
Lake District (pb)	1-85937-275-9	£9.99	Sherborne (pb)	1-85937-301-1	£9.99
Lancashire Living Memories	1-85937-335-6	£14.99	Shrewsbury (pb)	1-85937-325-9	£9.99
Lancaster, Morecambe, Heysham (pb)	1-85937-233-3	£9.99	Shropshire (pb)	1-85937-326-7	£9.99
Leeds (pb)	1-85937-202-3	£9.99	Shropshire Living Memories	1-85937-643-6	£14.99
Leicester (pb)	1-85937-381-x	£9.99	Somerset	1-85937-153-1	£14.99
Leicestershire & Rutland Living Memories	1-85937-500-6	£12.99	South Devon Coast	1-85937-107-8	£14.99
Leicestershire (pb)	1-85937-185-x	£9.99	South Devon Living Memories (pb)	1-85937-609-6	£9.99
Lighthouses	1-85937-257-0	£9.99	South East London (pb)	1-85937-263-5	£9.99
Lincoln (pb)	1-85937-380-1	£9.99	South Somerset	1-85937-318-6	£14.99
Lincolnshire (pb)	1-85937-433-6	£9.99	South Wales	1-85937-519-7	£14.99
Liverpool and Merseyside (pb)	1-85937-234-1	£9.99	Southampton (pb)	1-85937-427-1	£9.99
London (pb)	1-85937-183-3	£9.99	Southend (pb)	1-85937-313-5	£9.99
London Living Memories	1-85937-454-9	£14.99	Southport (pb)	1-85937-425-5	£9.99
Ludlow (pb)	1-85937-176-0	£9.99	St Albans (pb)	1-85937-341-0	£9.99
Luton (pb)	1-85937-235-x	£9.99	St Ives (pb)	1-85937-415-8	£9.99
Maidenhead (pb)	1-85937-339-9	£9.99	Stafford Living Memories (pb)	1-85937-503-0	£9.99
Maidstone (pb)	1-85937-391-7	£9.99	Staffordshire (pb)	1-85937-308-9	£9.99
Manchester (pb)	1-85937-198-1	£9.99	Stourbridge (pb)	1-85937-530-8	£9.99
Marlborough (pb)	1-85937-336-4	£9.99	Stratford upon Avon (pb)	1-85937-388-7	£9.99
Middlesex	1-85937-158-2	£14.99	Suffolk (pb)	1-85937-221-x	£9.99
Monmouthshire	1-85937-532-4	£14.99	Suffolk Coast (pb)	1-85937-610-x	£9.99
New Forest (pb)	1-85937-390-9	£9.99	Surrey (pb)	1-85937-240-6	£9.99
Newark (pb)	1-85937-366-6	£9.99	Surrey Living Memories	1-85937-328-3	£14.99
Newport, Wales (pb)	1-85937-258-9	£9.99	Sussex (pb)	1-85937-184-1	£9.99
Newquay (pb)	1-85937-421-2	£9.99	Sutton (pb)	1-85937-337-2	£9.99
Norfolk (pb)	1-85937-195-7	£9.99	Swansea (pb)	1-85937-167-1	£9.99
Norfolk Broads	1-85937-486-7	£14.99	Taunton (pb)	1-85937-314-3	£9.99
Norfolk Living Memories (pb)	1-85937-402-6	£9.99	Tees Valley & Cleveland (pb)	1-85937-623-1	£9.99
North Buckinghamshire	1-85937-626-6	£14.99	Teignmouth (pb)	1-85937-370-4	£7.99
North Devon Living Memories	1-85937-261-9	£14.99	Thanet (pb)	1-85937-116-7	£9.99
North Hertfordshire	1-85937-547-2	£14.99	Tiverton (pb)	1-85937-178-7	£9.99
North London (pb)	1-85937-403-4	£9.99	Torbay (pb)	1-85937-597-9	£9.99
North Somerset	1-85937-302-x	£14.99	Truro (pb)	1-85937-598-7	£9.99
North Wales (pb)	1-85937-298-8	£9.99	Victorian & Edwardian Dorset	1-85937-254-6	£14.99
North Yorkshire (pb)	1-85937-236-8	£9.99	Victorian & Edwardian Kent (pb)	1-85937-624-X	£9.99
Northamptonshire Living Memories	1-85937-529-4	£14.99	Victorian & Edwardian Maritime Album (pb)	1-85937-622-3	£9.99
Northamptonshire	1-85937-150-7	£14.99	Victorian and Edwardian Sussex (pb)	1-85937-625-8	£9.99
Northumberland Tyne & Wear (pb)	1-85937-281-3	£9.99	Villages of Devon (pb)	1-85937-293-7	£9.99
Northumberland	1-85937-522-7	£14.99	Villages of Kent (pb)	1-85937-294-5	£9.99
Norwich (pb)	1-85937-194-9	£8.99	Villages of Sussex (pb)	1-85937-295-3	£9.99
Nottingham (pb)	1-85937-324-0	£9.99	Warrington (pb)	1-85937-507-3	£9.99
Nottinghamshire (pb)	1-85937-187-6	£9.99	Warwick (pb)	1-85937-518-9	£9.99
Oxford (pb)	1-85937-411-5	£9.99	Warwickshire (pb)	1-85937-203-1	£9.99
Oxfordshire (pb)	1-85937-430-1	£9.99	Welsh Castles (pb)	1-85937-322-4	£9.99
Oxfordshire Living Memories	1-85937-525-1	£14.99	West Midlands (pb)	1-85937-289-9	£9.99
Paignton (pb)	1-85937-374-7	£7.99	West Sussex (pb)	1-85937-607-x	£9.99
Peak District (pb)	1-85937-280-5	£9.99	West Yorkshire (pb)	1-85937-201-5	£9.99
Pembrokeshire	1-85937-262-7	£14.99	Weston Super Mare (pb)	1-85937-306-2	£9.99
Penzance (pb)	1-85937-595-2	£9.99	Weymouth (pb)	1-85937-209-0	£9.99
Peterborough (pb)	1-85937-219-8	£9.99	Wiltshire (pb)	1-85937-277-5	£9.99
Picturesque Harbours	1-85937-208-2	£14.99	Wiltshire Churches (pb)	1-85937-171-x	£9.99
Piers	1-85937-237-6	£17.99	Wiltshire Living Memories (pb)	1-85937-396-8	£9.99
Plymouth (pb)	1-85937-389-5	£9.99	Winchester (pb)	1-85937-428-x	£9.99
Poole & Sandbanks (pb)	1-85937-251-1	£9.99	Windsor (pb)	1-85937-333-x	£9.99
Preston (pb)	1-85937-212-0	£9.99	Wokingham & Bracknell (pb)	1-85937-329-1	£9.99
Reading (pb)	1-85937-238-4	£9.99	Woodbridge (pb)	1-85937-498-0	£9.99
Redhill to Reigate (pb)	1-85937-596-0	£9.99	Worcester (pb)	1-85937-165-5	£9.99
Ringwood (pb)	1-85937-384-4	£7.99	Worcestershire Living Memories	1-85937-489-1	£14.99
Romford (pb)	1-85937-319-4	£9.99	Worcestershire	1-85937-152-3	£14.99
Royal Tunbridge Wells (pb)	1-85937-504-9	£9.99	York (pb)	1-85937-199-x	£9.99
Salisbury (pb)	1-85937-239-2	£9.99	Yorkshire (pb)	1-85937-186-8	£9.99
Scarborough (pb)	1-85937-379-8	£9.99	Yorkshire Coastal Memories	1-85937-506-5	£14.99
Sevenoaks and Tonbridge (pb)	1-85937-392-5	£9.99	Yorkshire Dales	1-85937-502-2	£14.99
Sheffield & South Yorks (pb)	1-85937-267-8	£9.99	Yorkshire Living Memories (pb)	1-85937-397-6	£9.99

See Frith books on the internet at www.francisfrith.co.uk

FRITH PRODUCTS & SERVICES

Francis Frith would doubtless be pleased to know that the pioneering publishing venture he started in 1860 still continues today. Over a hundred and forty years later, The Francis Frith Collection continues in the same innovative tradition and is now one of the foremost publishers of vintage photographs in the world. Some of the current activities include:

Interior Decoration

Today Frith's photographs can be seen framed and as giant wall murals in thousands of pubs, restaurants, hotels, banks, retail stores and other public buildings throughout the country. In every case they enhance the unique local atmosphere of the places they depict and provide reminders of gentler days in an increasingly busy and frenetic world.

Product Promotions

Frith products are used by many major companies to promote the sales of their own products or to reinforce their own history and heritage. Frith promotions have been used by Hovis bread, Courage beers, Scots Porage Oats, Colman's mustard, Cadbury's foods, Mellow Birds coffee, Dunhill pipe tobacco, Guinness, and Bulmer's Cider.

Genealogy and Family History

As the interest in family history and roots grows world-wide, more and more people are turning to Frith's photographs of Great Britain for images of the towns, villages and streets where their ancestors lived; and, of course, photographs of the churches and chapels where their ancestors were christened, married and buried are an essential part of every genealogy tree and family album.

Frith Products

All Frith photographs are available Framed or just as Mounted Prints and Posters (size 23 x 16 inches). These may be ordered from the address below. From time to time other products - Address Books, Calendars, Table Mats, etc - are available.

The Internet

Already fifty thousand Frith photographs can be viewed and purchased on the internet through the Frith websites and a myriad of partner sites.

For more detailed information on Frith companies and products, look at these sites:

www.francisfrith.co.uk
www.francisfrith.com
(for North American visitors)

See the complete list of Frith Books at:

www.francisfrith.co.uk

This web site is regularly updated with the latest list of publications from the Frith Book Company. If you wish to buy books relating to another part of the country that your local bookshop does not stock, you may purchase on-line.

For further information, trade, or author enquiries please contact us at the address below:
The Francis Frith Collection, Frith's Barn, Teffont, Salisbury, Wiltshire, England SP3 5QP.
Tel: +44 (0)1722 716 376 Fax: +44 (0)1722 716 881 Email: sales@francisfrith.co.uk

See Frith books on the internet at www.francisfrith.co.uk

HOW TO ORDER YOUR FREE MOUNTED PRINT
and other Frith prints at half price

Mounted Print
Overall size 14 x 11 inches

*Fill in and cut out this voucher and return it
with your remittance for £2.25 (to cover
postage and handling to UK addresses).
For overseas addresses please include £4.00
post and handling.
Choose any photograph included in this book.
Your SEPIA print will be A4 in size. It will be
mounted in a cream mount with a burgundy
rule line (overall size 14 x 11 inches).*

Order additional Mounted Prints
at HALF PRICE (only £7.49 each*)
If you would like to order more Frith prints
from this book, possibly as gifts for friends
and family, you can buy them at half price
(with no additional postage and handling
costs).

Have your Mounted Prints framed
For an extra £14.95 per print* you can have
your mounted print(s) framed in an elegant
polished wood and gilt moulding, overall
size 16 x 13 inches (no additional postage
and handling required).

---

* IMPORTANT!

**These special prices are only available if you
order at the same time as you order your free
mounted print. You must use the ORIGINAL
VOUCHER on this page (no copies permitted).
We can only despatch to one address.**

Voucher for **FREE** and Reduced Price *Frith Prints*

*Please do not photocopy this voucher. Only the original is valid,
so please fill it in, cut it out and return it to us with your order.*

Picture ref no	Page number	Qty	Mounted @ £7.49	Framed + £14.95	Total Cost
		1	Free of charge*	£	£
			£7.49	£	£
			£7.49	£	£
			£7.49	£	£
			£7.49	£	£
			£7.49	£	£
Please allow 28 days for delivery			* Post & handling (UK)	£2.25	
			Total Order Cost	£	

Title of this book . . . .

I enclose a cheque/postal order for £ . . . .
made payable to 'The Francis Frith Collection'

OR please debit my Mastercard / Visa / Switch / Amex card
(credit cards please on all overseas orders), details below

Card Number

Issue No (Switch only)   Valid from (Amex/Switch)

Expires   Signature

Name Mr/Mrs/Ms . . . .
Address . . . .
. . . .
. . . .
. . . . Postcode . . . .
Daytime Tel No . . . .
Email . . . .

Valid to 31/12/05

Send completed Voucher form to:
The Francis Frith Collection, Frith's Barn, Teffont, Salisbury, Wiltshire SP3 5QP

Free Print – see overleaf

Would you like to find out more about Francis Frith?

We have recently recruited some entertaining speakers who are happy to visit local groups, clubs and societies to give an illustrated talk documenting Frith's travels and photographs. If you are a member of such a group and are interested in hosting a presentation, we would love to hear from you.

Our speakers bring with them a small selection of our local town and county books, together with sample prints. They are happy to take orders. A small proportion of the order value is donated to the group who have hosted the presentation. The talks are therefore an excellent way of fundraising for small groups and societies.

Can you help us with information about any of the Frith photographs in this book?

We are gradually compiling an historical record for each of the photographs in the Frith archive. It is always fascinating to find out the names of the people shown in the pictures, as well as insights into the shops, buildings and other features depicted.

If you recognize anyone in the photographs in this book, or if you have information not already included in the author's caption, do let us know. We would love to hear from you, and will try to publish it in future books or articles.

Our production team

Frith books are produced by a small dedicated team at offices in the converted Grade II listed 18th-century barn at Teffont near Salisbury, illustrated above. Most have worked with the Frith Collection for many years. All have in common one quality: they have a passion for the Frith Collection. The team is constantly expanding, but currently includes:

Jason Buck, John Buck, Douglas Mitchell-Burns, Ruth Butler, Heather Crisp, Isobel Hall, Maureen Harrison, Julian Hight, Peter Horne, James Kinnear, Karen Kinnear, Tina Leary, David Marsh, Sue Molloy, Kate Rotondetto, Dean Scource, Eliza Sackett, Terence Sackett, Sandra Sampson, Adrian Sanders, Sandra Sanger, Julia Skinner, Lewis Taylor, Shelley Tolcher, and Lorraine Tuck.